Body Positive Pride Zine July 2019

Body Positive Pride Zine

©LOUD & QUEER and Chris Mok Creations 2019   Chris Mok & Marisa Wohlschlaeger

Creator & Model
Chris Mok @cmok1224

Marisa Wohlschlaeger
@marisatherainbow &
Model
Allison Wilson
Ben Mendoza @_benmichaels_
Betty Bangs @betty_bangs
Danielle Jackson @Baltimorestateofmind
Ellie Webb @red_princess_ellie
Hannah @hannahbethjuarez
Kaytee @Kaytee
Kelsey Daniels @andsheshere_
Kendra Sitton @pskendraaa
Kevin Terry Lee @kevtlee
M Valladolid @mvalladolid1
Revi Britton @ReviBritton
Sabrina Johnson @bubbblysabrina
Stephanie Aleman @stephanie.aleman.sd
Tamala S. Baker @tamala.s.baker
Tanisha Campbell
Teena Acree @Iamteenamaree
Make Up Artist & Model
Carlito Beal
Lilly @Lilianaxrendon
Model, Photography, Make Up
Naya Marie Velazco @Everythingyouownyoustillowe
Photographer
Brandon Pease @Photobps
Darin Fong @darinfongphotography
Dennis Rosenberg @dennis_rosenberg_photography
Brand
FTM Essentials @ftmessentials
Rainbow And Co @rainbowandcouk
Sissy Boy @sissyboyclothing

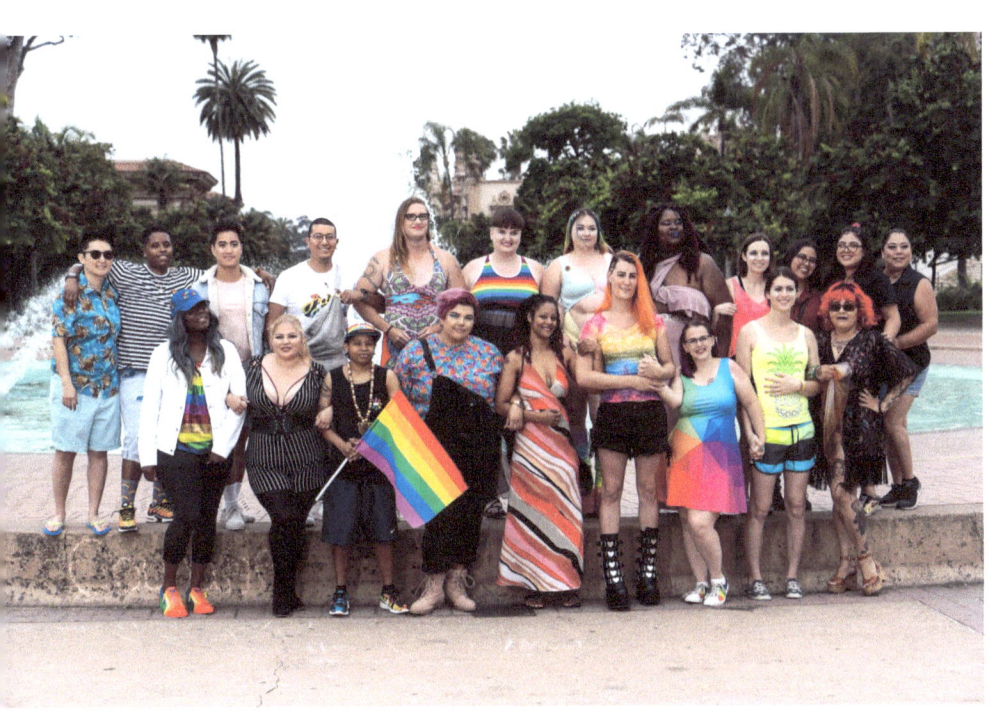

CONTENT WARNING: This zine contains strong language and nudity. View with caution

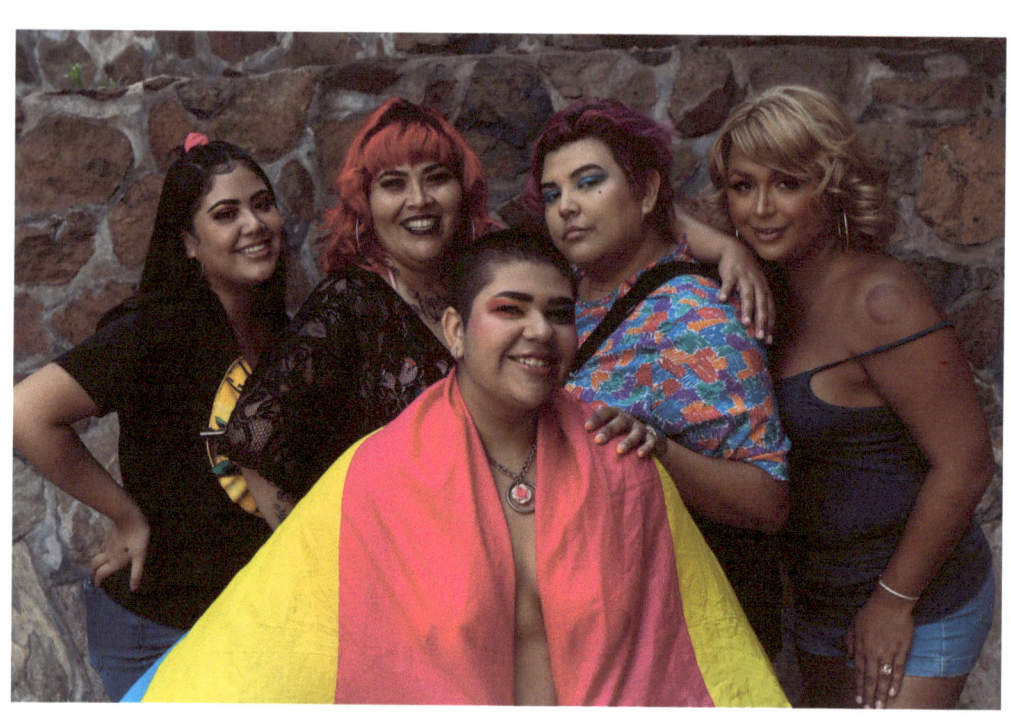

Models: Liliana Rendon, Betty Bangs, Carlito Beal, Naya Marie Velazco, M. Valladolid
Photographer: Darren Rosenberg

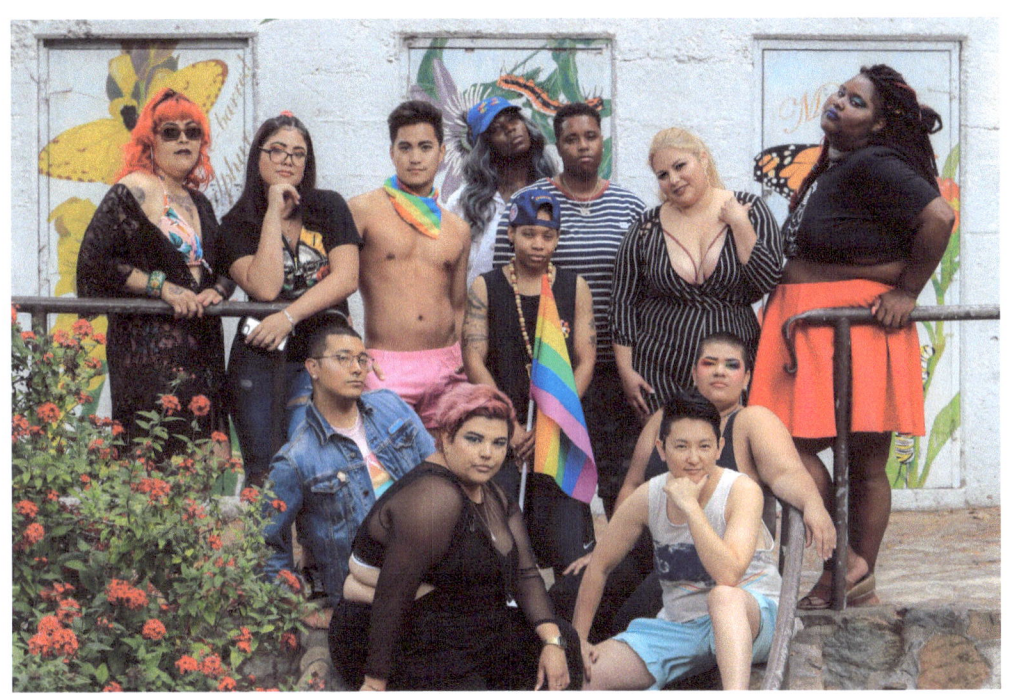

"Not being ashamed of who you are inside and out. Being comfortable in your own skin. I celebrate my pride by being unapologetically me and being happy and accepting of who I am in a world that not everyone will welcome it. I'm black, a female, and a lesbian in the military. The repeal of DADT (Don't Ask Don't Tell) meant everything to me. No longer having to worry about getting processed out based on my sexuality was such a huge relief because I love doing what I do even though some days are challenging than others."

-Tamala S. Baker

Models: Betty Bangs, Liliana Rendon, Kevin Lee, Teena Acree, Danielle Jackson, Stephanie Aleman, Kelsey Olivia, Ben Mendoza, Carlito Beal, Tamala Baker, Chris Mok, M. Valladolid

Photographer: Brandon Pease

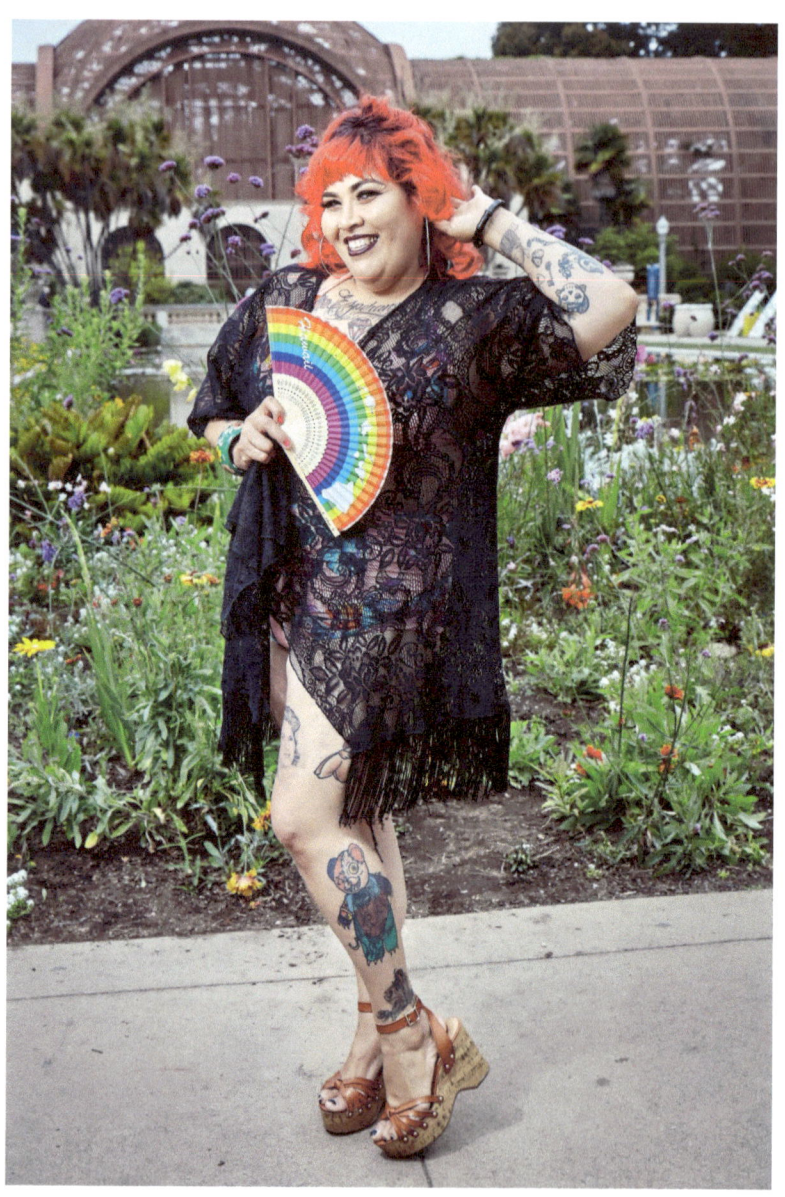

"Body positive means love yourself, your body. You're perfect the way you are. All shapes and sizes are beautiful!"
-Betty Bangs

Model: Betty Bangs
Photographer: Darin Fong

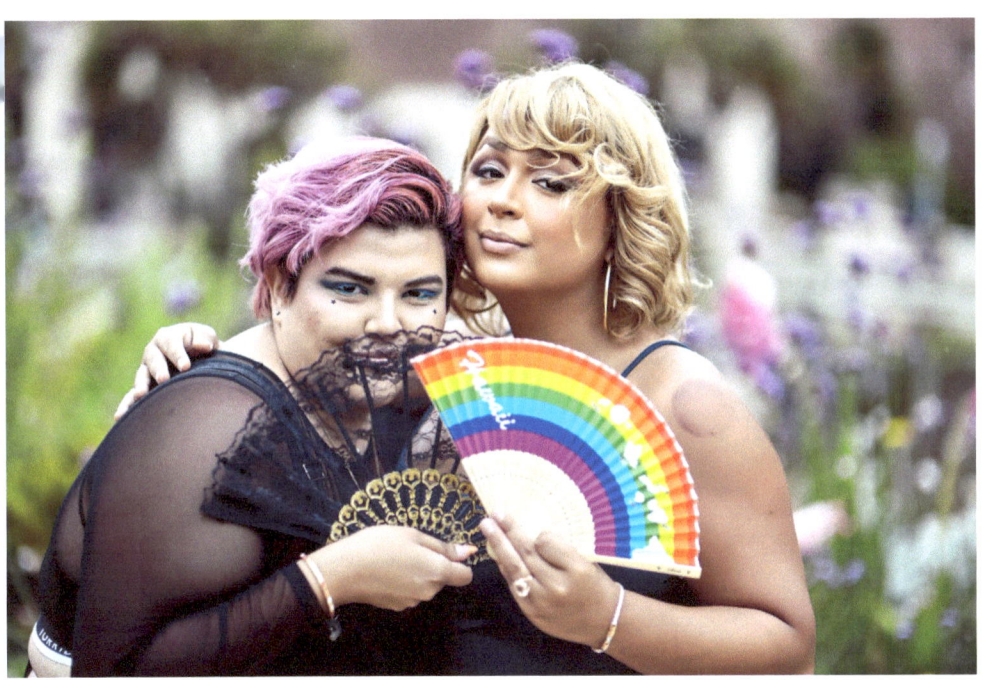

Models: Carlito Beal, Naya Marie Velazco
Photographer: Darin Fong

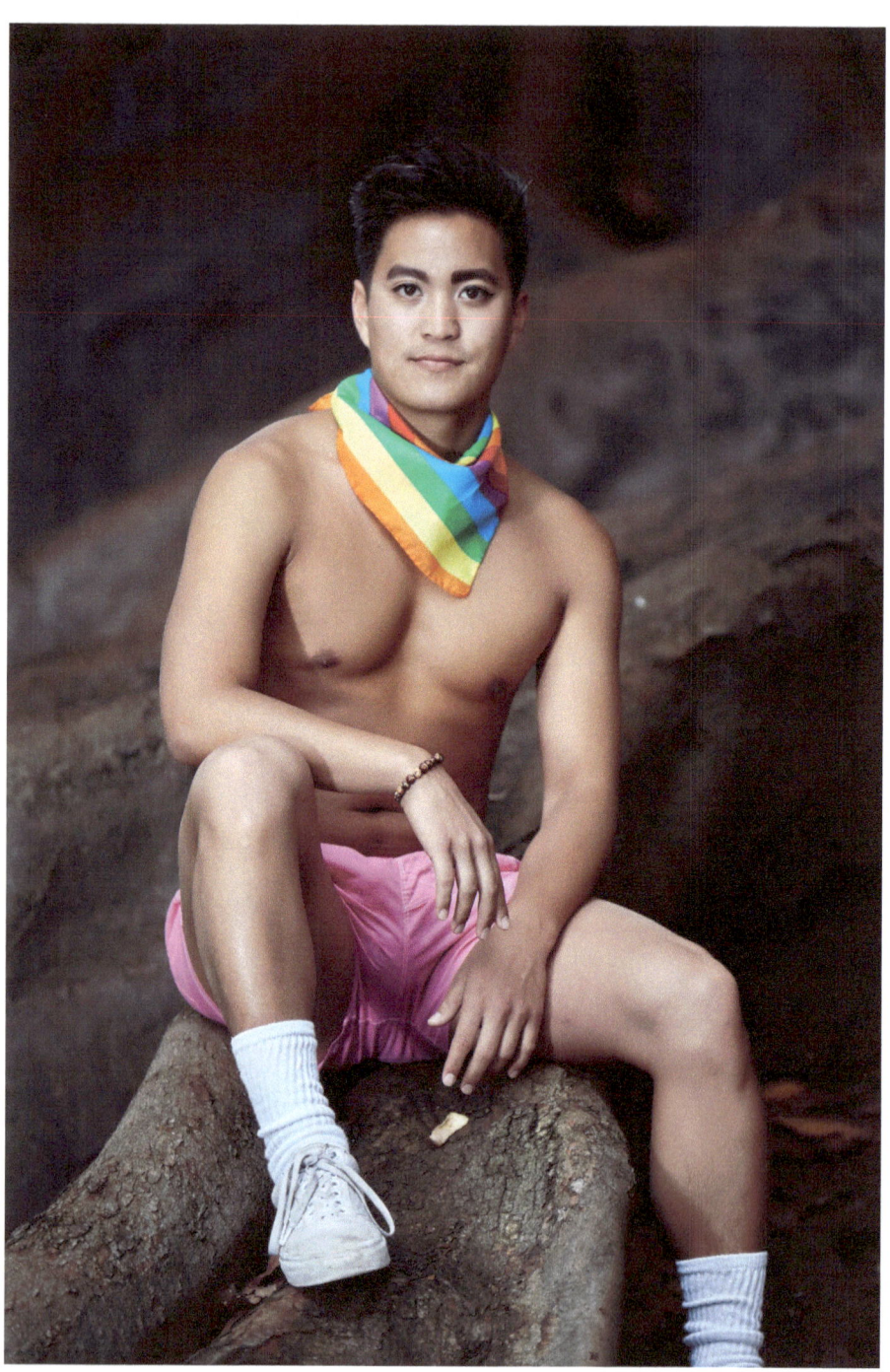

Model: Kevin Terry Lee
Photographer: Darin Fong

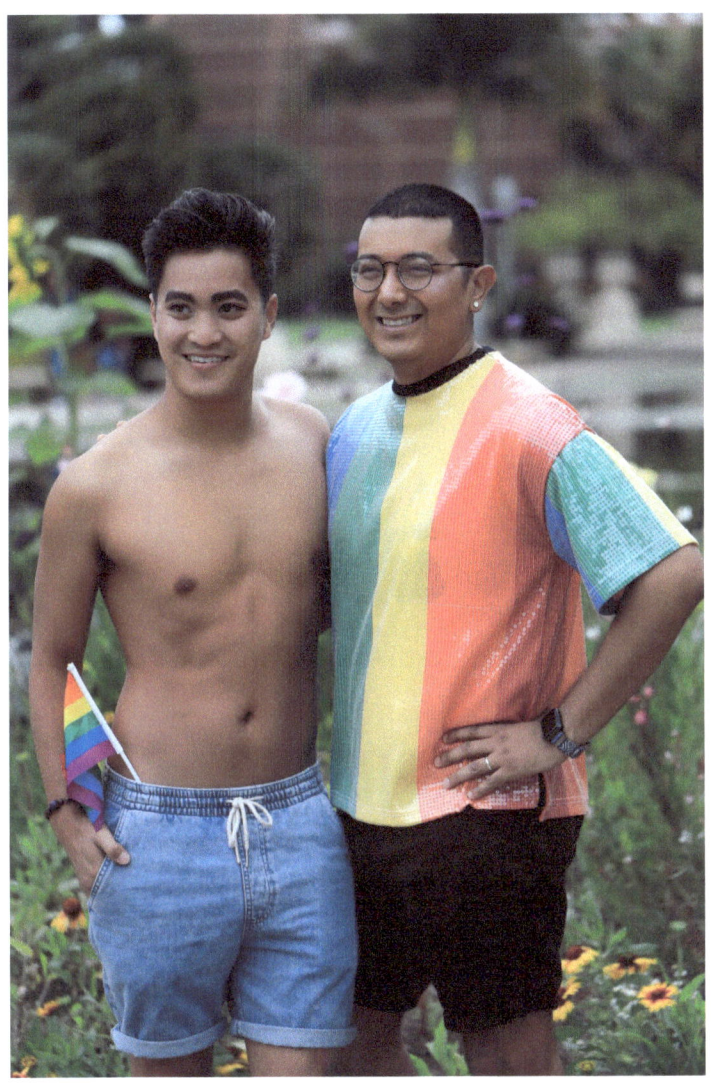

"Body positivity is a revolution. We get to dictate our own beauty standards. For me, it means being comfortable within my own skin. It is being self-aware and intentional about how I want to live. And when I can do all that, it means that I can be proud of who I am, as well as the uniqueness I bring to the world. My body is perfect. I can choose to keep it the way it is right now, or I can choose to change it - whatever form it's in, I add more beauty to the world and communities I live in."
-Kevin Terry Lee

Model: Kevin Terry Lee & Ben Mendoza   Photographer: Brandon Pease

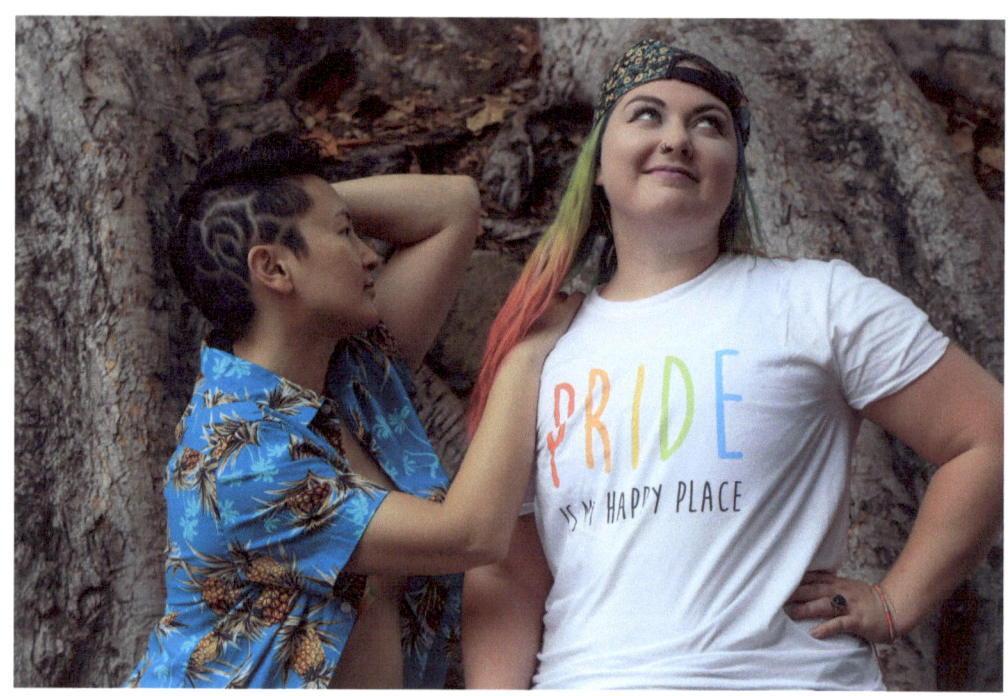

"Loving myself has been a lifelong struggle. So many messages about my body and myself permeated my young life and created obstacles between my true self and me. In living authentically and surrounding myself with a community that understands me, I have changed 100%. I feel empowered and beautiful being seen by a community that loves and values me as I am: Queer, Nonbinary, and beautiful."
-Marisa Wohlschlaeger

Model: Chris Mok, Marisa Wohlschlaeger
Photographer: Brandon Pease
Brand: Rainbow And Co

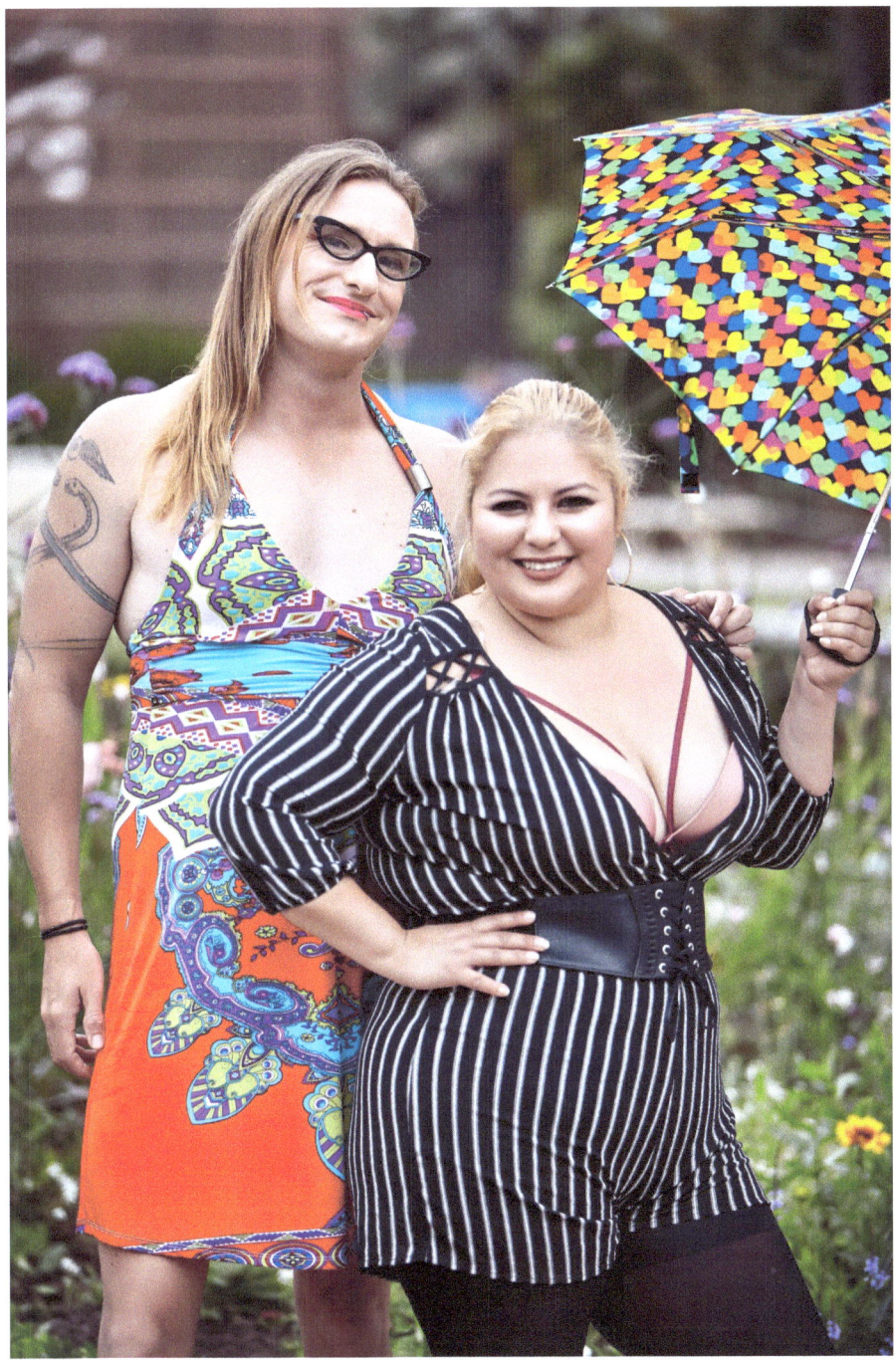

Model: Ellie Webb, Stephanie Aleman — Photographer: Darin Fong

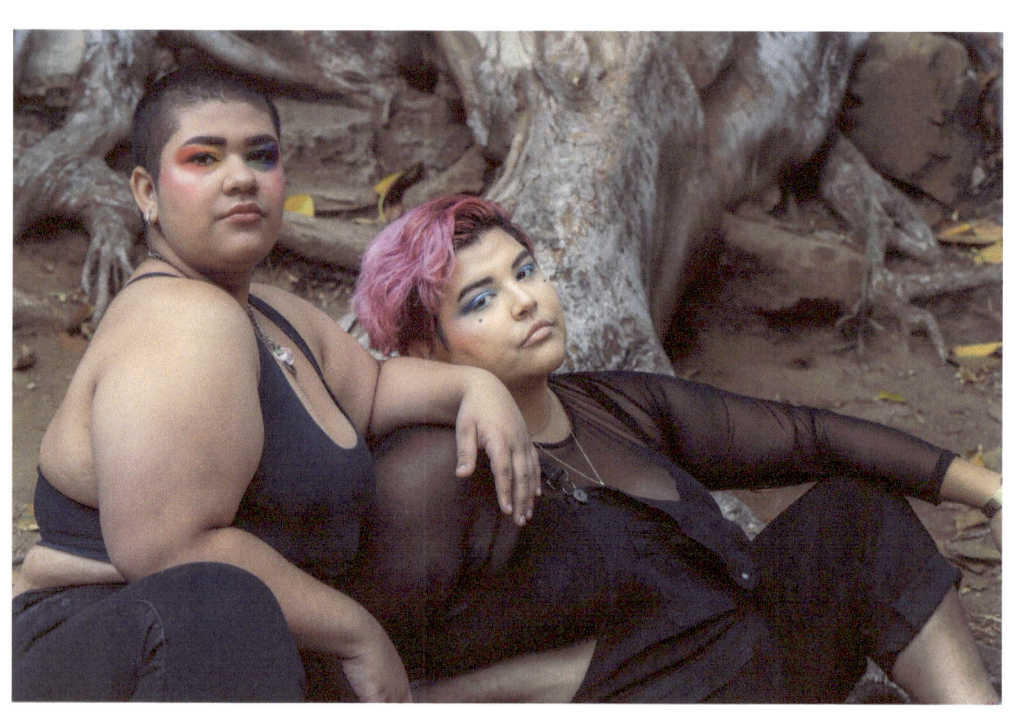

Model: M Valladolid, Carlito Beal
Photographer: Brandon Pease

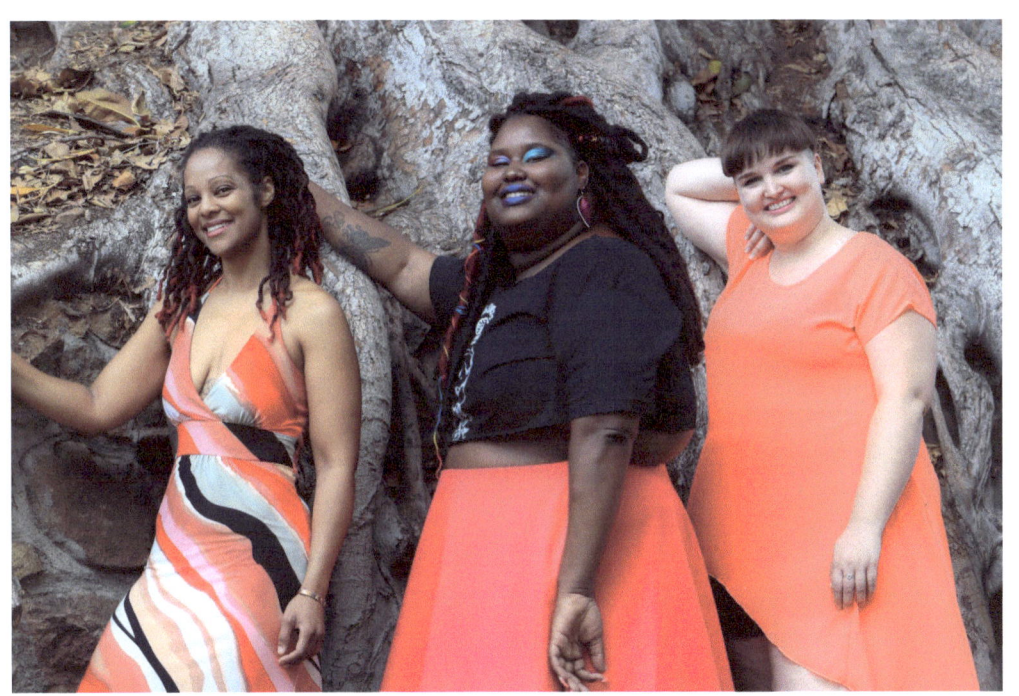

"Body positivity has been key in my journey of accepting my queerness. Until I became present in my body, I was able to push down my attraction to women and other gender expressions. Disassociating was how I coped for so long, so accepting my body then listening to it is how I finally realized my true identity. The shame I internalized for so long about my body and my sexual identity is one of the reasons I celebrate Pride today. Pride combats those messages of hate so I can live in a place where I accept myself and surround myself with accepting people."

-Kendra Sitton

Model: Tanisha Campbell, Kelsey Daniels, Kendra Sitton   Photographer: Brandon Pease

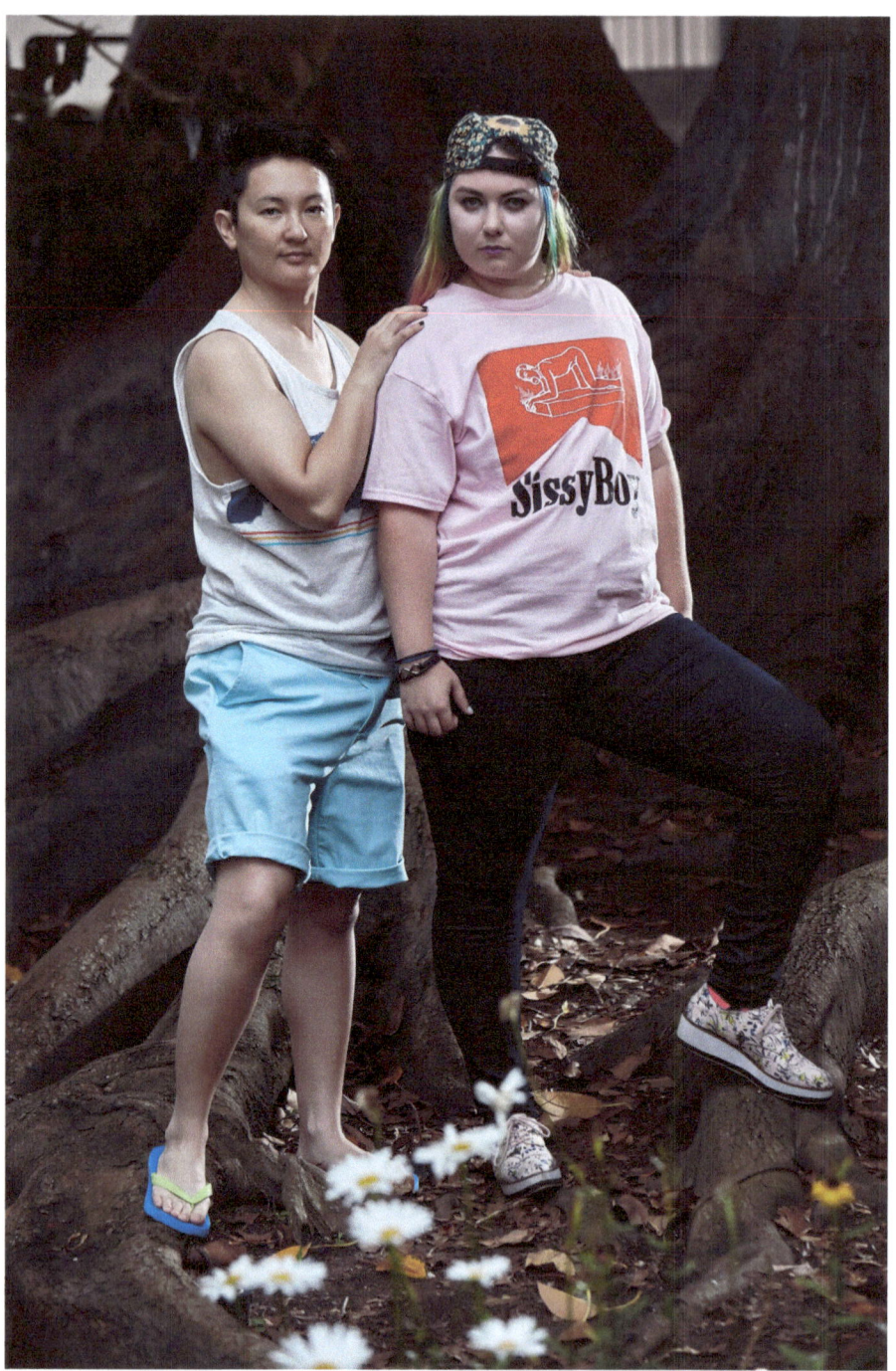

Model: Chris Mok, Marisa Wohlschlaeger
Photographer: Darin Fong
Brand: Sissy Boy, FTM Essentials

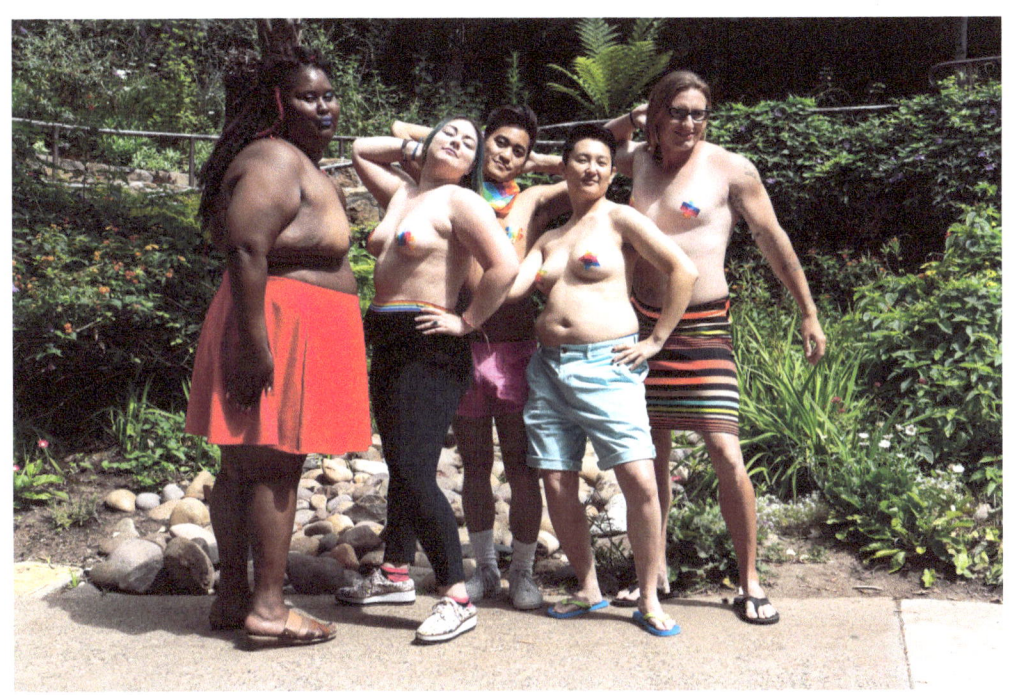

"I believe in body neutrality and fat liberation. I understand that my relationship with my body constantly changes but I am deserving of all of the things regardless. I also know that we have to acknowledge that fatphobia and white supremacy lend themselves to the idea that I or those with bodies like mine shouldn't exist in our bodies."
-Kelsey Daniels

Model: Marisa Wohlschlaeger, Kevin Terry Lee, Chris Mok, Ellie Webb
Photographer: Darin Fong

Body Positive Pride Zine — July 2019

Be true,
Be YOU!

©LOUD & QUEER and Chris Mok Creations 2019 — Chris Mok & Marisa Wohlschlaeger

Body Positive Pride Zine   September 2019

TO THE FRONT!

Zine

©LOUD & QUEER and Chris Mok Creations 2019   Chris Mok & Marisa Wohlschlaeger

Creator & Model
Chris Mok @cmok1224
Marisa Wohlschlaeger @marisatherainbow & @loudandqueerzine

Model
Bias Collins @llamaguccii
Dyani Amo Melgarejo @LostBird
Kelsey Olivia @andsheshere_
Jessica Polanco @jessyourlooks
Nyisha @nyishageedoublu
Hung Real Lo @hungreallo

Make Up Artist
Carlito Espudo @alittlemanly_

Photographer
Naya Marie Velazco @Everythingyouownyoustillowe
Fiona Stone #missfreudianslit
Millie Lawyer @thingsthroughlenses
Sarah Ann @telescopicpoetry

Brand
Project No Labels @projectnolabels
Trans Guy Supply @transguysupply
Starship Soliz @starship_soliz

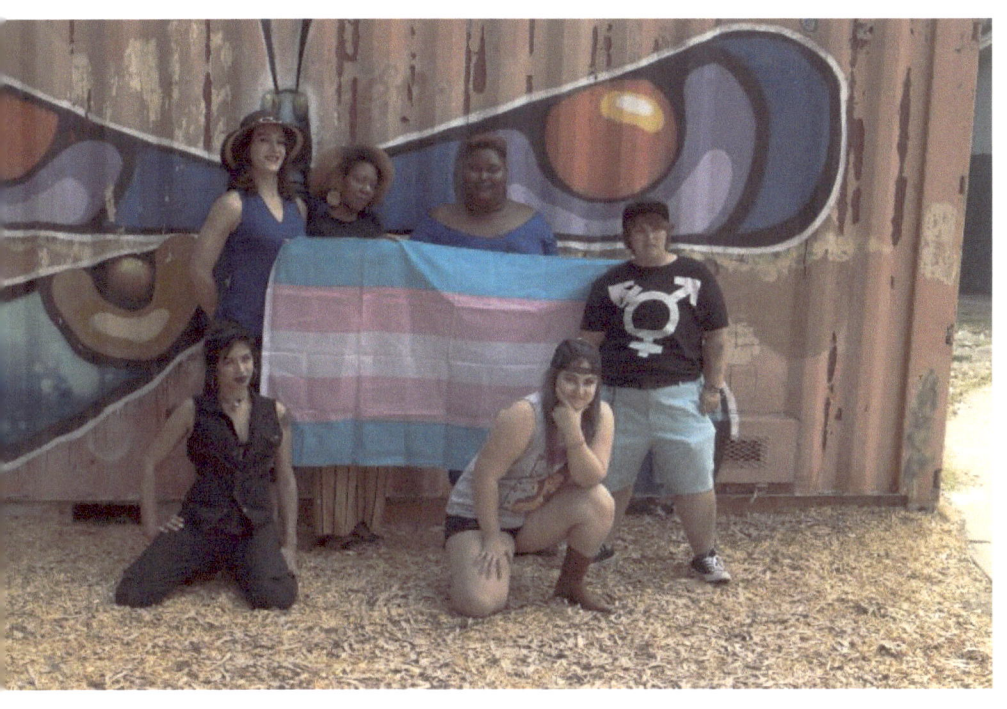

CONTENT WARNING: This zine contains strong language and nudity. View with caution

Photographer: Fiona Stone

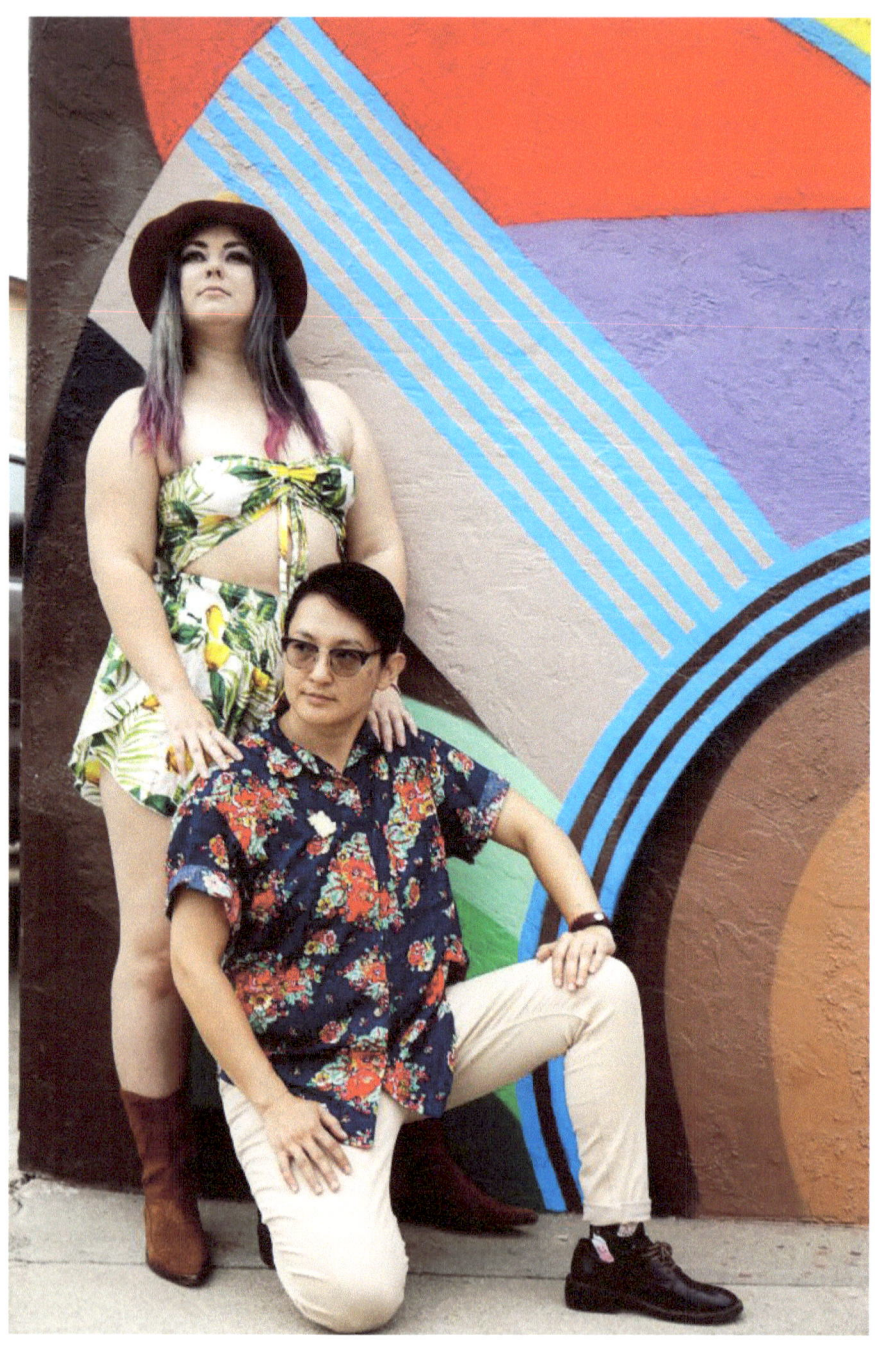

Models: Chris Mok, Marisa Wohlschlaeger
Photographer: Sarah Ann

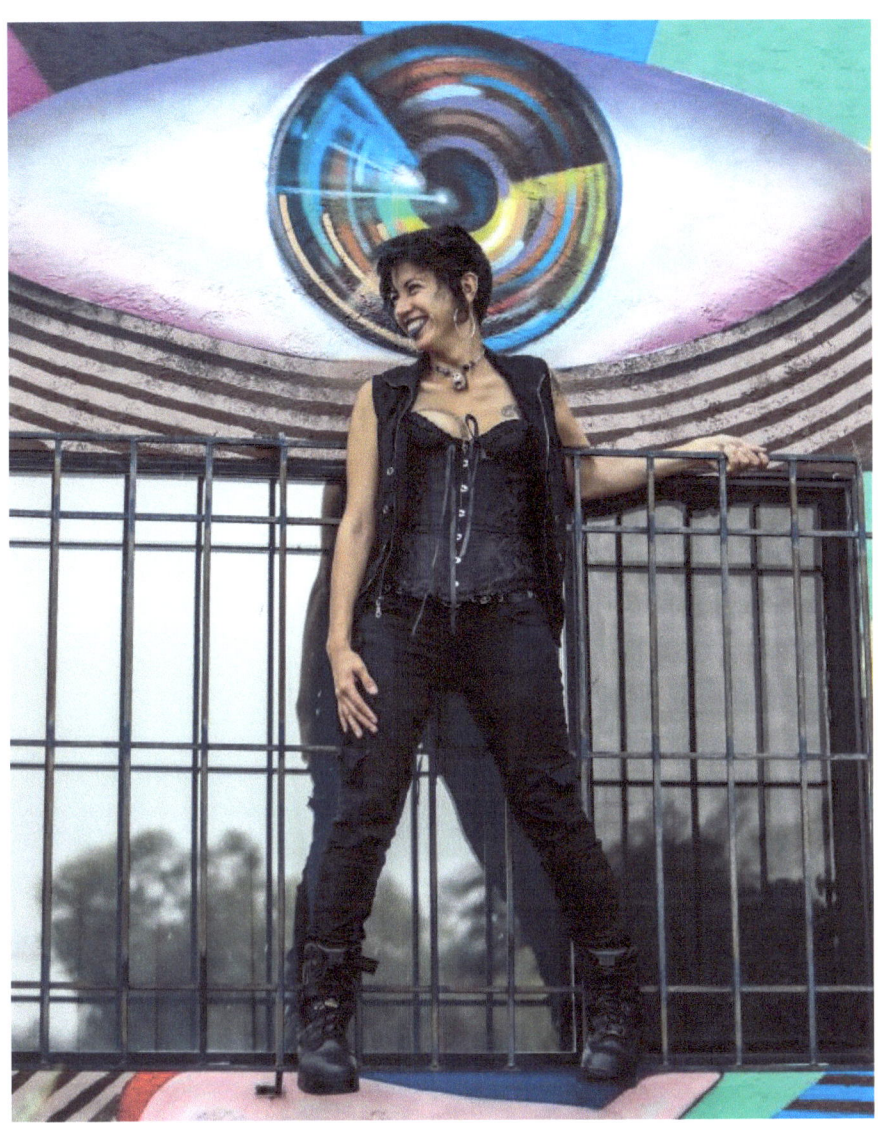

"Body positivity is truly experiencing the human form as an individual work of art. The space we occupy, our shape, our melanin, our hairiness or hairlessness, every curve, scar, freckle, zit, tattoo, bruise, wrinkle, all of this makes our canvas. Our actions tell our true story. Every human has a story of survival, told through the weathering of our skin. To me, that is beautiful."

-Dyani Amo Melgarejo

Model: Dyani Amo Melgarejo
Photographer: Millie Lawyer

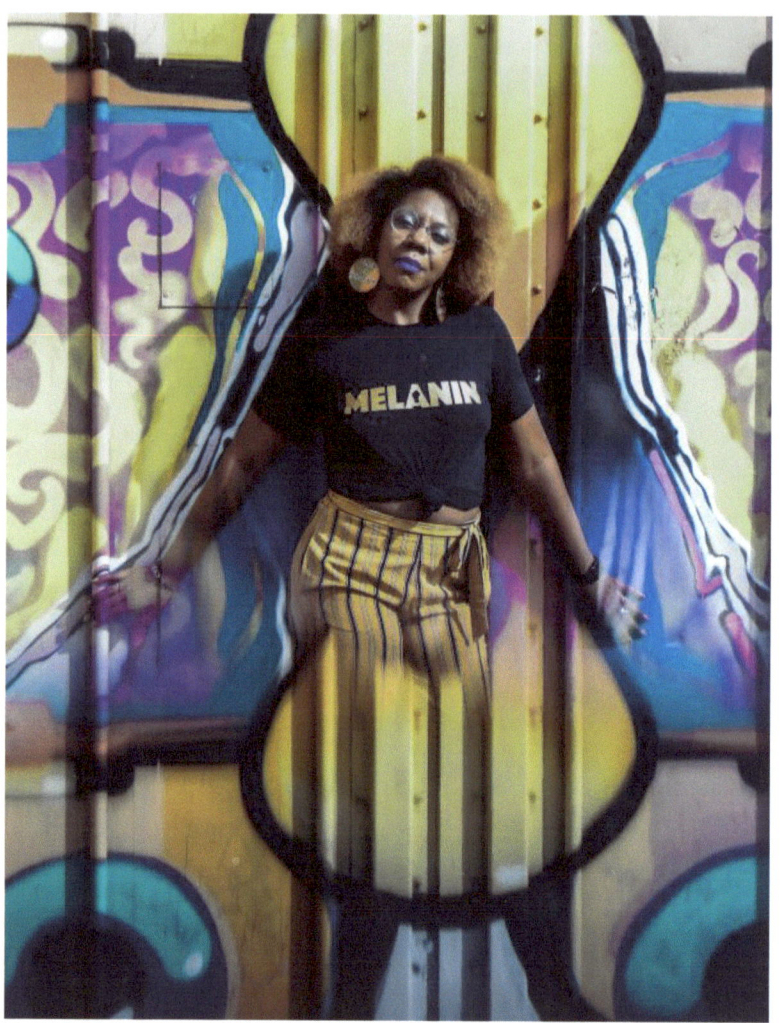

"Honestly, this is the first year that I have actually been publicly 'out' about being asexual. As a cishet person, I never want to take up space in the LGBTQIA+ community, but it is this community who told me me this year that I do belong. That the A is for me! It is difficult to explain to folks what that looks like, especially because the visibility of black asexual folks is slim to none in the media. In addition, Black womxn's sexuality and bodies have historically been hypersexualized, so it is hard for people to wrap their head around someone who looks like me to not be a sexual person."
-Nyisha

Model: Nyisha
Photographer: Millie Lawyer

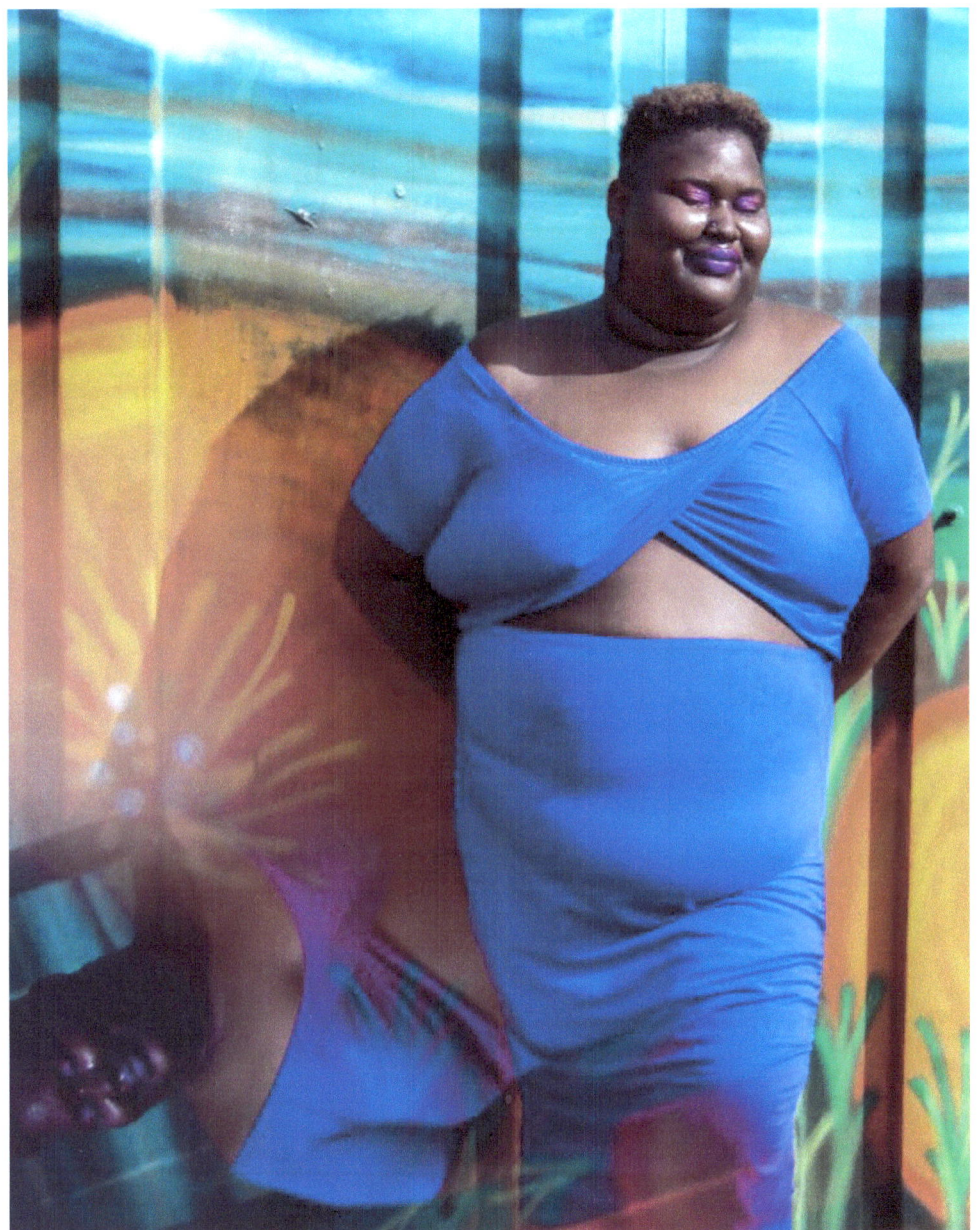

"Being queer to me means believing in the possibility of there being more than a one size fits all life."
-Kelsey Marie

Models: Kelsey Marie
Photographer: Millie Lawyer

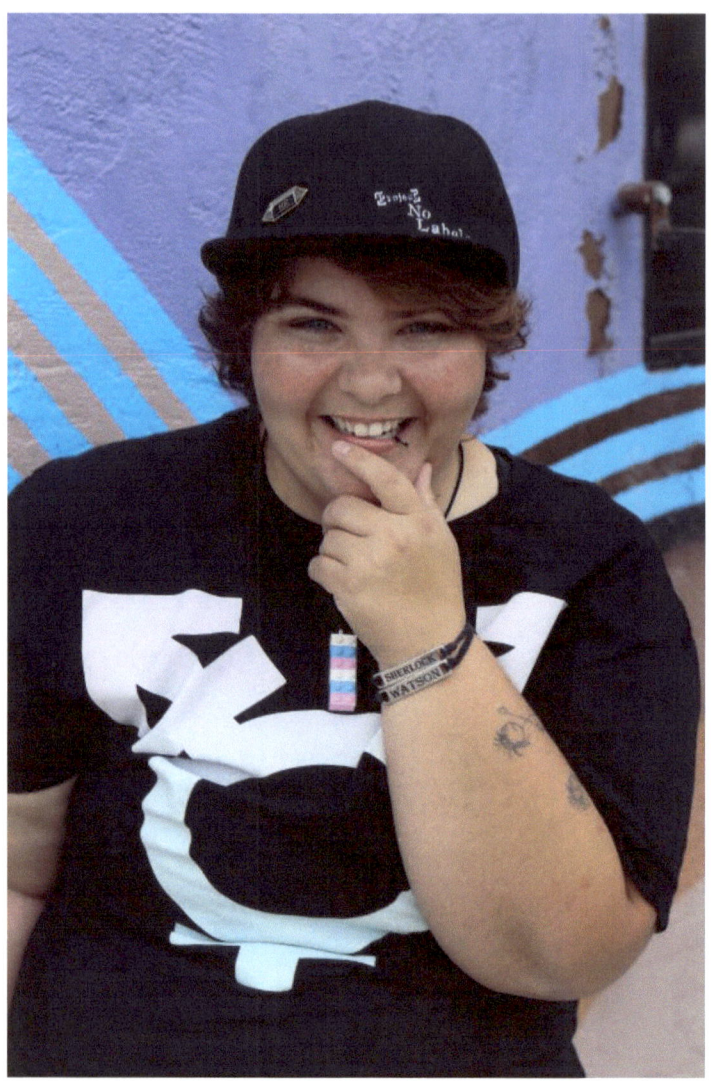

"Being LGBTQIA+ means I'm more aware of myself and others as fluid people who cannot be confined to labels that weren't ever made to truly serve them. Being trans-masculine, but short, squat, and pre-surgery, my body doesn't conform to traditional 'maleness.' This gives me an opportunity to show people that men are men regardless of how 'feminine' their bodies may appear. Being neurodivergent is also an important part of my identity. I am bipolar and have other mental health conditions as well. I'm thankful for the perspectives these conditions have given me and the opportunity I've had to grow through serious and continual self-reflection."

Model: Bias Collins
Photographer: Naya Marie Velazco
Brand: Project No Labels

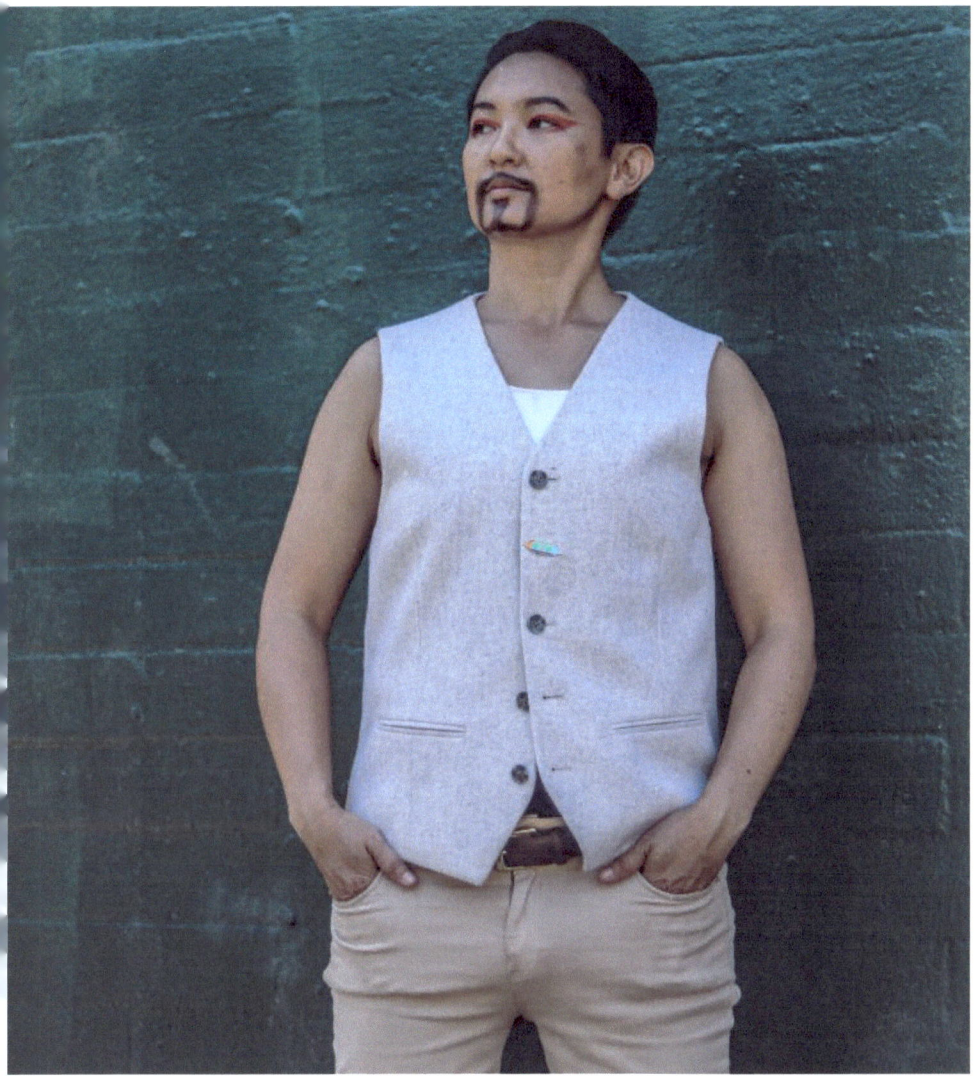

Chris Mok is a pansexy non-binary trans masculine magic making queerdo human of color.

They/He anoints themself as Hung Real Lo to discover his inner truth.

Hung Real Lo has been centering both performance and self discovery since first taking the stage in Oakland in 2008. He has been blessing San Diego venues since his initial appearance in the September 2018 Trans Pride Fundraiser.

Sir Lo constantly strives to be a visible performer and inspiration at the intersection of multi-faceted identities and personal liberation. –Hung Real Lo

Model: Hung Real Lo   Photographer: Fiona Stone

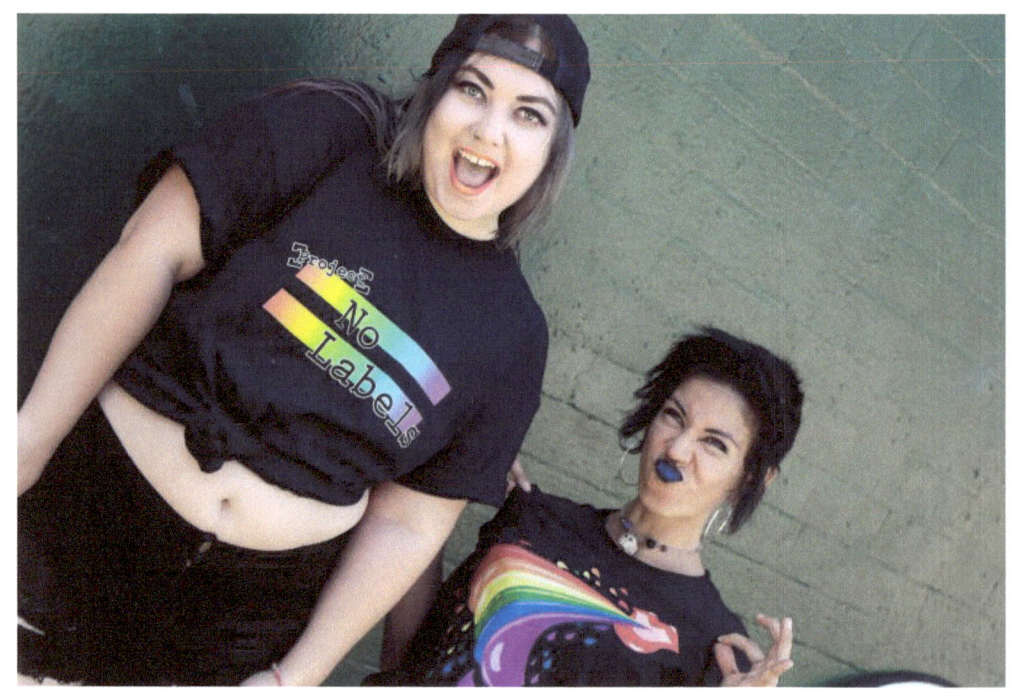

"Being LGBTQIA+ to me means creating my own narrative that's unique in contrast to a heteronormative world that is still widely unaccepting of our community. It means rebelling against social norms and giving a big "f@%k you" and middle finger to the majority of people who'd rather us not be here. It means we get to choose our "family" and create a community of love and acceptance our biological families may have failed to give us."

-Steven, Creator of Starship Soliz

Model: Marisa Wohlschlaeger, Dyani Amo Melgarejo
Photographer: Chris Mok
Brand: Project No Labels, Starship Soliz

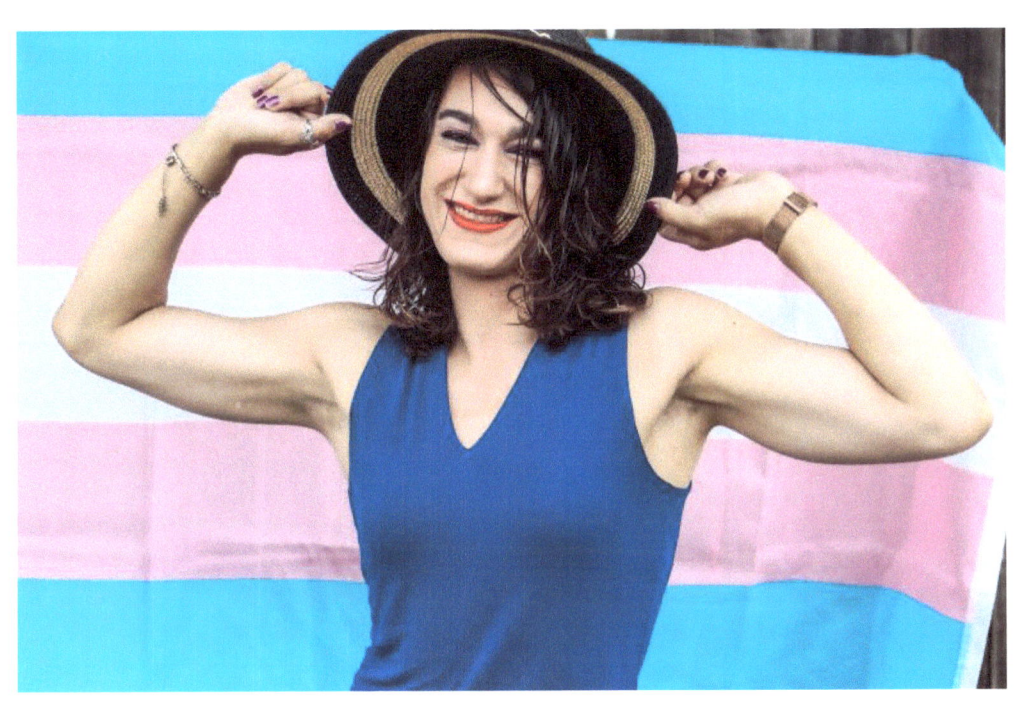

Model: Jessica Polanco
Photographer: Millie Lawyer

The photographers

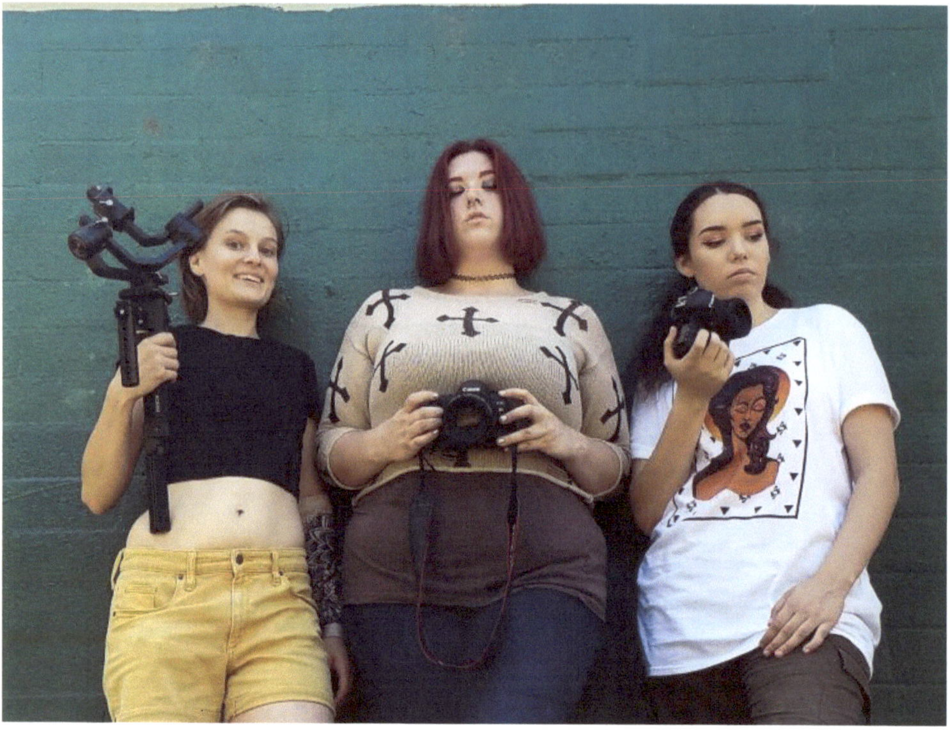

Sarah Ann, Fiona Stone, Millie Lawyer, Naya Marie Velazco (not pictured)

The Brands

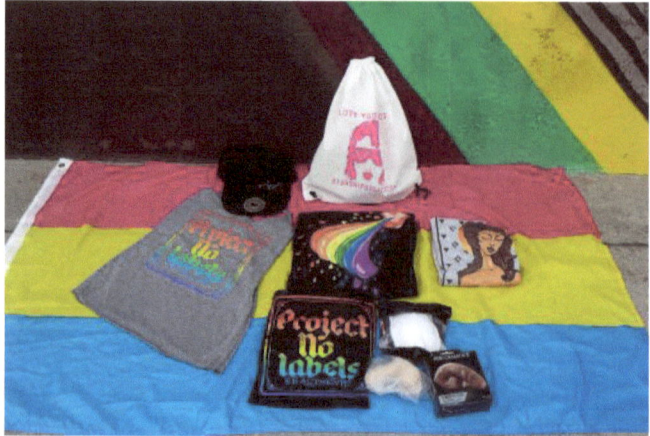

Project No Labels, Trans Guy Supply, Starship Soliz

www.ingramcontent.com/pod-product-compliance
Lightning Source LLC
Chambersburg PA
CBHW040348220526
45473CB00009B/2811